THIS BOOK BELONGS TO

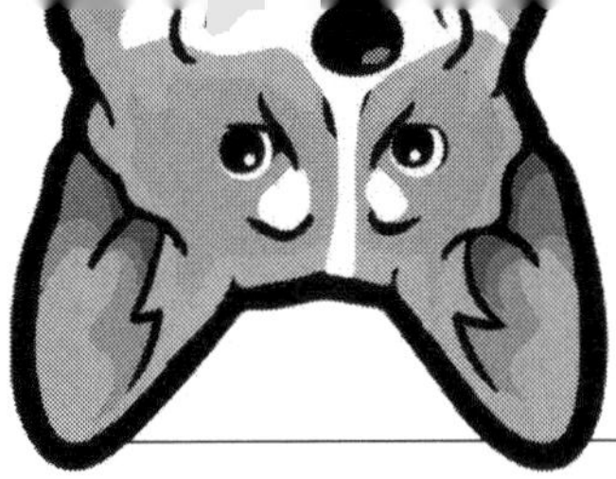

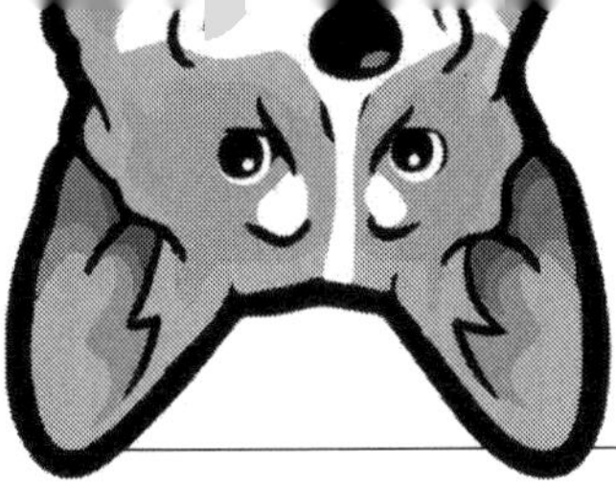

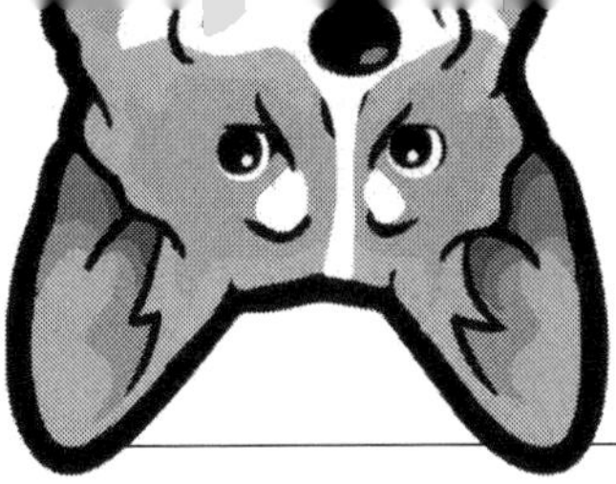

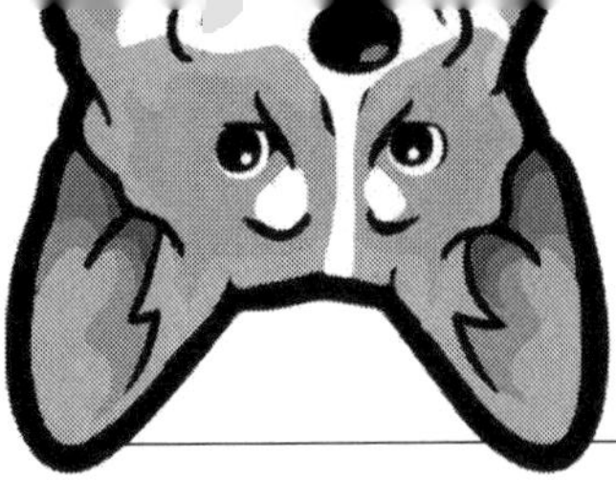

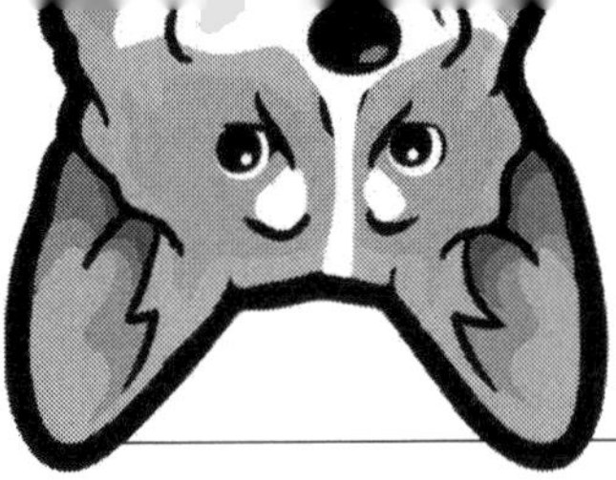

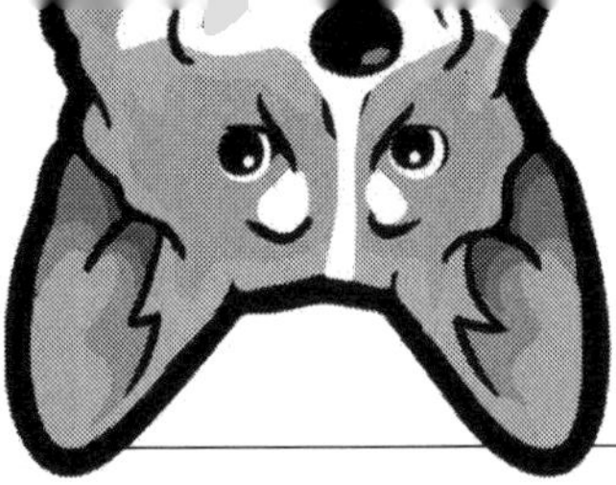

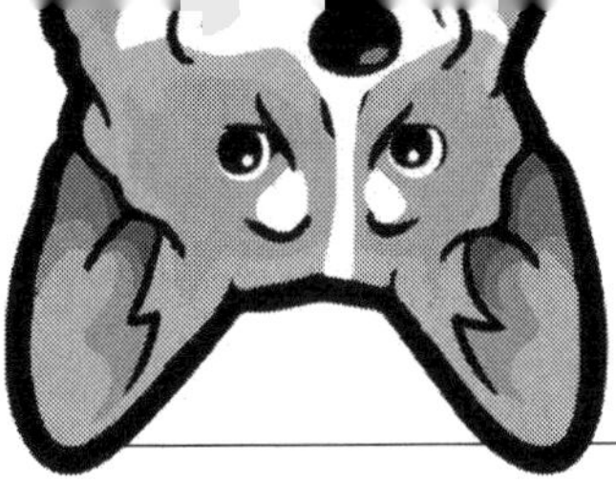

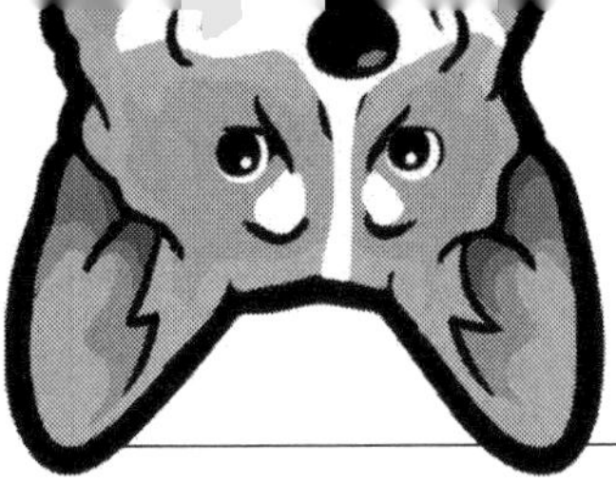

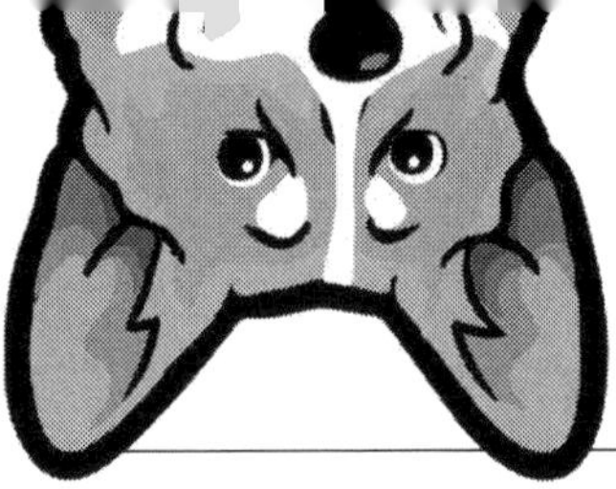

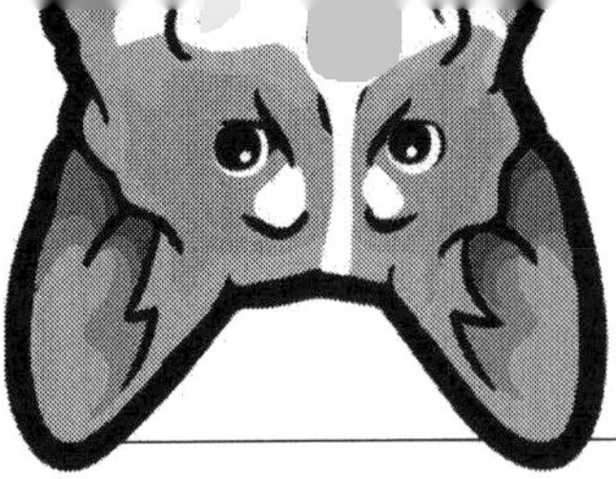

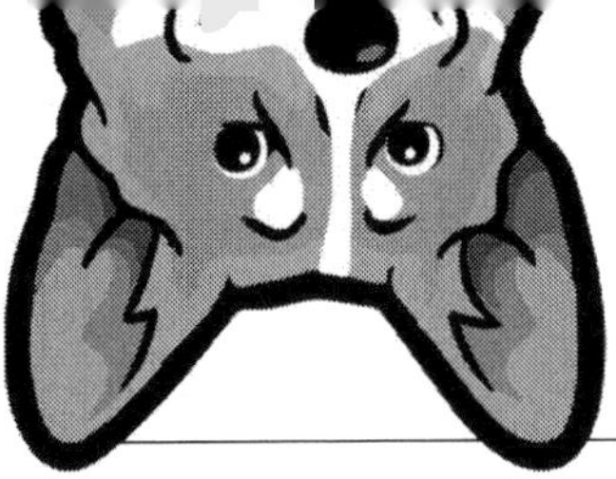

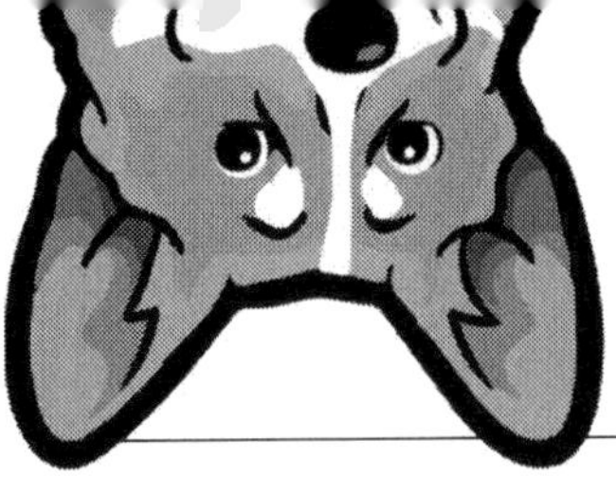

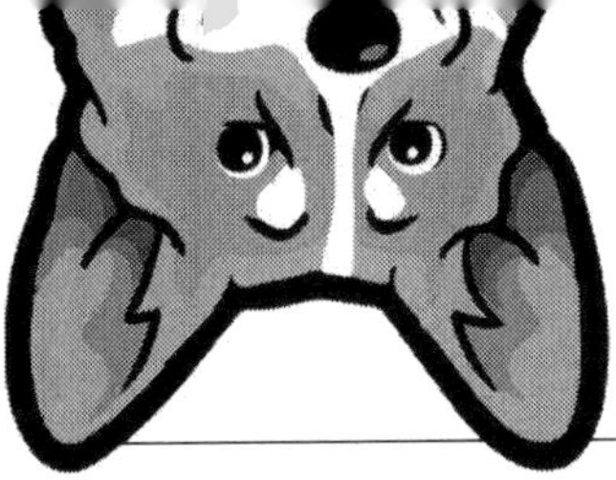

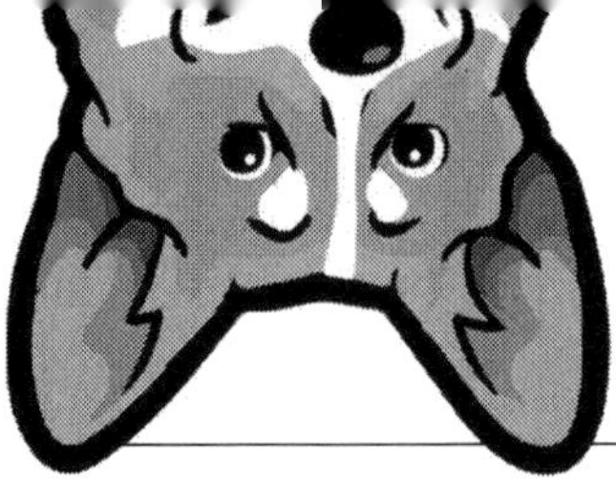

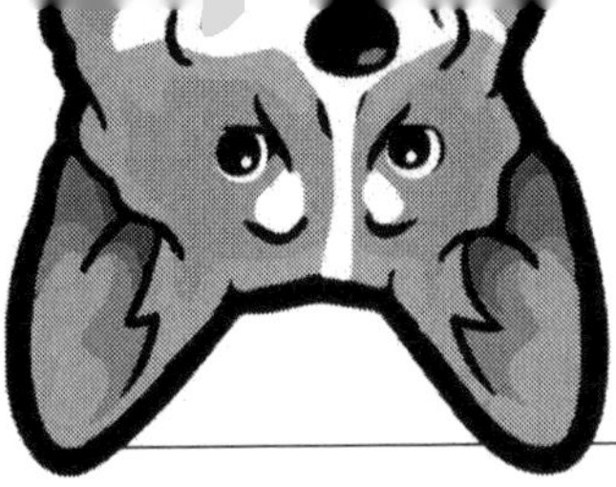

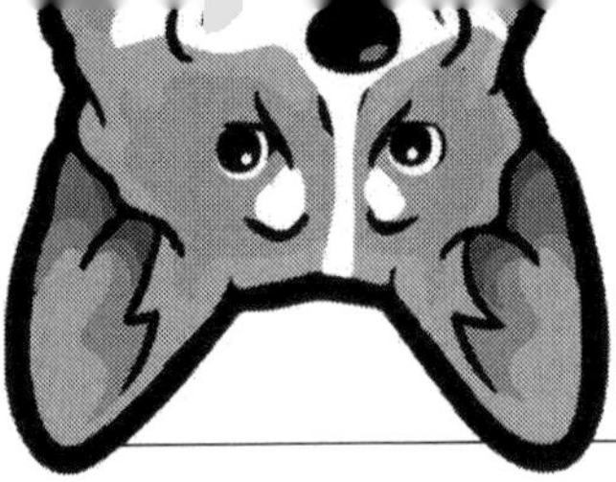

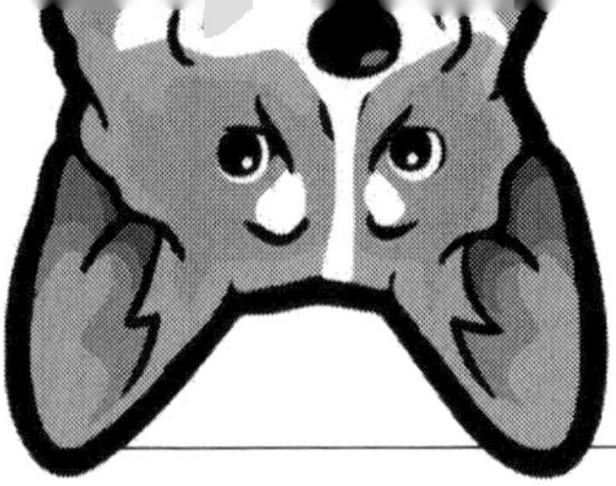

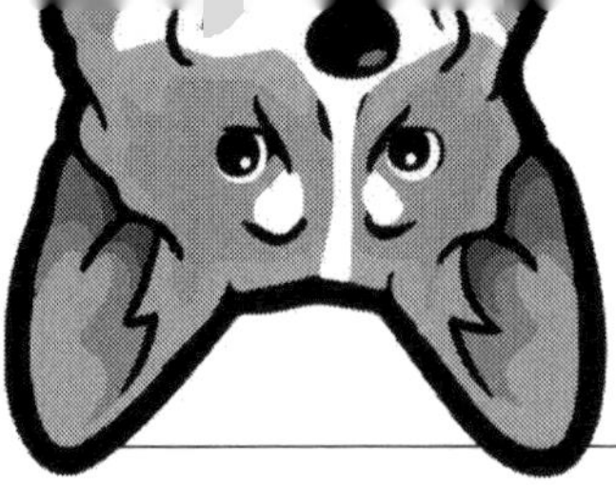

Made in the USA
Coppell, TX
13 July 2023

19152287R00061